W9-DCA-828

FREDERICK DOUGLASS
The LAST DAY *of* SLAVERY

written by WILLIAM MILLER • *illustrated by* CEDRIC LUCAS

LEE & LOW BOOKS Inc.   New York

Text copyright © 1995 by William Miller
Illustrations copyright © 1995 by Cedric Lucas
All rights reserved. No part of this book may be reproduced
by any means without the written permission of the publisher.
LEE & LOW BOOKS Inc., 95 Madison Avenue, New York, NY 10016
Printed in Hong Kong by South China Printing Co. (1988) Ltd.
10 9 8 7 6 5 4 3 2 1
Book production and design by Our House

The text is set in Baskerville.
The illustrations are rendered in pastel on paper that has
been treated with pumice and gesso.

Library of Congress Cataloging-in-Publication Data
Miller, William
Frederick Douglass: the last day of slavery/by William Miller;
illustrated by Cedric Lucas. — 1st ed.
p. cm.
ISBN 1-880000-42-3 (paperback)
1. Douglass, Frederick, 1817?-1895—Childhood and youth—Juvenile literature.
2. Fugitive slaves—Maryland—Biography—Juvenile literature.
[1. Douglass, Frederick, 1817?-1895—Childhood and youth.
2. Afro-Americans—Biography.   3. Fugitive slaves.]
I. Lucas, Cedric, ill.   II. Title.
E449.D75M55   1995
973.8'092—dc20   94-26542
[B] CIP AC

For Sterling Watson and Peter Meinke,
with gratitude
—W.M.

To Diane, Jorrell, and Jaleesa,
and to all who inspire
—C.L.

Frederick Douglass was born a slave.

He never knew his father and saw his mother only a few times. She walked all night through freezing woods, across fields burned white by the moon.

She walked all night just to hold him.
Frederick remembered her face for the rest of his life: dark skin and warm eyes, a mouth that broke into a loving smile.

His grandmother raised Frederick. She told him that he would not see his mother again, that the slave master had sold her to another plantation many miles away.

Frederick tried to understand, but when he thought of his mother, tears and more tears came into his eyes.

He soon learned that even children were expected to work in the fields. Walking behind the grownups, he pulled weeds that grew between the corn rows.

Only on Saturday was he allowed a few hours of play. But Frederick was shy and didn't care for the children's games. He thought about his mother, why she had to go away. He wondered why he was a slave, why the master was the master.

All around him, Frederick saw frightened
people: men and women who walked with their

heads down, who never spoke above a whisper
when the overseer was nearby.

But still the overseer would beat them.
Once, Frederick saw him whip the master's
favorite slave. The old man had overslept,

forgotten to groom the master's prize stallion.
Frederick felt the blows on his back, on the back
of all the slaves who stood beside him.

At night, when he lay beside the fire, Frederick planned to escape. He dreamed of running away to the north, to the cities where black people had no fear of whites. He dreamed of stealing a boat, rowing down the river to the sea, rowing all the way to New York.

But all Frederick could do was dream.

The master expected more of him as he grew older,
stronger. Sometimes, in the fall, Frederick worked in the

fields until midnight. The first light of dawn found him
back in the same row of corn or cotton.

When Frederick was seventeen a new man came to the plantation—a slave breaker named Covey.

His job was to break the spirit of any man or woman who tried to escape, who longed to be free.

The breaker saw that Frederick was not like the others. He liked being alone, reading on the grass whenever the slaves were given a rest. He knew that Frederick had to be broken soon, before he taught other slaves to read, to think for themselves.

And so the breaker worked him, twice as hard as any man on the plantation. Even when he sat down to eat his lunch, Covey watched him with a cold eye.

One day, Frederick was working in the tobacco barn.
It was a hot day, and he soon grew tired. Dizzy and sick,
he stumbled out into the light, fell down beneath an oak
tree. The breaker told Frederick to get up and finish his

work. Frederick tried to explain, but Covey wouldn't listen.

Frederick felt the blow of a hickory stick against his head. The breaker hit him again and again, until he crawled into the barn.

That night Frederick ran away. He hid in the woods and ate wild berries, drank water from a shallow stream.

He knew he would be beaten or even killed if he returned. He had never felt such pain or loneliness before.

Lying in the dark of the woods, he wished he were an animal: a creature with fur and claws to protect himself. He wished he were a bird, able to soar over the treetops, fly on the wind as far as the sea.

When the sun came up, Frederick heard someone walking toward him. He was about to run when he saw a fellow slave, a kind man named Sandy. Frederick told him about the beating, and Sandy took him in. In front of the fire, he cleaned Frederick's wounds, gave him Indian corn to eat.

Sandy knew the magic of Africa—spells and charms their
people brought to America on slave ships. He gave Frederick a
magic root that would protect him from the breaker's whip.

Frederick wanted to believe in magic, anything
that would save his life.

When he returned to the plantation, the breaker called him to the whipping post.

Frederick saw the anger in Covey's eyes and knew no magic would save him now. He knew that any man—slave or free—had to defend himself.

The breaker struck him across the chest with his knotted whip.

Frederick raised his arm to stop the second blow and the fight began.

While they kicked and hit each other, while they
wrestled in the dirt, the slaves watched in disbelief.

They had never seen a slave defend himself. They
had never seen such courage.

When the fight was over, the breaker looked at Frederick with new eyes. Fear was in his eyes, but also respect. Frederick knew that Covey would never strike him again. He would never admit that a slave had fought back—a slave he couldn't break.

That night, while he lay by the fire, Frederick thought
about his mother. He remembered how she had walked
all night, across the frozen fields, just to hold him.
  He told himself that he would never think or act
like a slave again. He promised his mother that one day

he would escape, that all slaves would be free.

Frederick looked up into the sky and saw the moon drifting through the clouds.

After the moon came a star, pale and far off, but burning in the sky.

AUTHOR'S NOTE

Frederick Douglass was born a slave in 1817. He never knew his father and saw his mother only a few times before her death. He was encouraged to learn to read by his master's wife. His passion for books and learning was born at this time and lasted throughout his life.

In 1838, Frederick escaped to the north. He gained fame as a speaker in the anti-slavery movement. In 1845, he published *The Narrative of the Life of Frederick Douglass: An American Slave.* This book, perhaps more than any other, helped American society understand the cruelty of slavery.

Frederick wrote more volumes of his autobiography in later years and continued his struggle for the freedom of his people until his death in 1895.